Watching Orangutans

in Asia

Deborah Underwood

www.heinemann.co.uk/library

Visit our website to find out more information about Heinemann Library books.

To order:

☎ Phone 44 (0) 1865 888066

▤ Send a fax to 44 (0) 1865 314091

▣ Visit the Heinemann Bookshop at www.heinemann.co.uk/library to browse our catalogue and order online.

First published in Great Britain by Heinemann Library, Halley Court, Jordan Hill, Oxford OX2 8EJ, part of Harcourt Education. Heinemann is a registered trademark of Harcourt Education Ltd.

© Harcourt Education Ltd 2006
First published in paperback in 2007
The moral right of the proprietor has been asserted.

Editorial: Nancy Dickmann and Sarah Chappelow
Design: Ron Kamen and edesign
Illustrations: Martin Sanders
Picture Research: Maria Joannou and Christine Martin
Production: Camilla Crask
Originated by Modern Age
Printed and bound in Italy by Printer Trento srl

13 digit ISBN 978 0 431 19085 3 (HB)
10 digit ISBN 0 431 19085 2 (HB)
10 09 08 07 06
10 9 8 7 6 5 4 3 2 1

13 digit ISBN 978 0 431 19088 4 (PB)
10 digit ISBN 0 431 19088 7 (PB)
11 10 09 08 07
10 9 8 7 6 5 4 3 2 1

British Library Cataloguing in Publication Data

Underwood, Deborah
Watching orangutans in Asia. - (Wild world)
599.8'83
A full catalogue record for this book is available from the British Library.

Acknowledgments

The author and publisher are grateful to the following for permission to reproduce copyright material: Ardea pp. 5 (Adrian Warren), 7 (Jean Paul Ferrero), 17 (M. Watson), 20 (Masahiro Iijima); Corbis p. 27; FLPA pp. 4 (Konrad Wthe/Minden Pictures), 11 (Mark Newman), 24 (Frans Lanting/Minden Pictures); Nature Picture Library pp. 10 (Anup Shah), 12 (Anup Shah), 14 (Anup Shah), 15 (Anup Shah), 16 (Anup Shah), 18 (Ingo Arndt), 19 (Anup Shah), 23 (Anup Shah), 25 (Anup Shah), 26 (Mark Linfield); NPHA pp. 8, 9 (Nick Garbutt), 22; Steve Bloom p. 21; Still Images p. 13. Cover photograph of a mother orangutan and baby reproduced with permission of Nature Picture Library (Anup Shah).

The publishers would like to thank Michael Bright of the BBC Natural History Unit for his assistance in the preparation of this book.

Contents

Words written in bold, **like this**, are explained in the glossary.

Meet the orangutans

This is Asia, the home of orangutans. Long ago, people gave these apes the name *orang hutan*. These words mean "person of the forest".

▶▶ *It is easy to see why some people once thought orangutans were human.*

Orangutans belong to the **great ape** family. Like all great apes, they are very clever. Chimpanzees and gorillas are also great apes.

Orangutans are related to gorillas like this one.

Island homes

Borneo and Sumatra are large **islands** near the **continent** of Asia. Orangutans used to live all over Southeast Asia. Now they only live here.

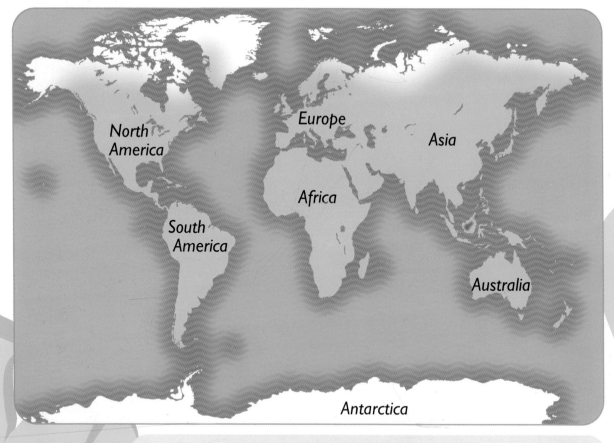

North America

Europe

Asia

Africa

South America

Australia

Antarctica

Key ● *This colour shows where orangutans live in Asia.*

The islands are near the **equator**. The weather here is warm and damp. The Sun shines for twelve hours each day. Heavy rains fall for part of the year.

▲ *Borneo and Sumatra have only two seasons: rainy and dry.*

7

Rainforests

Orangutans live in **rainforests**. Trees reach up to the sky. Their thick leaves block the Sun's rays. Very little light reaches the forest floor.

▶▶ *Rainforests give orangutans many kinds of food to eat.*

*▲ Orangutans share the rainforest
with many plants and animals.*

The rainforest is home to thousands of
different animals. Some live on the forest
floor. Others live high in the trees.

There's an orangutan!

Orangutans often hang from the trees. Their long red hair helps them blend into the shadows.

▶▶ *Orangutans are shorter than most humans, but much stronger.*

long arms

toes for gripping

red hair

Orangutans have long arms, long hands, and long feet. They can grasp branches with their toes. **Males** are more than twice as big as **females**.

◀◀ *Full-grown males have cheek pads.*

On the move

Orangutans pull themselves from tree to tree. They are heavy, so they move carefully. They make sure each branch can hold their weight.

▼ *Baby orangutans hold on tight as they are carried through the trees.*

Orangutans use their hands and feet to grab branches.

When an orangutan cannot reach the next tree, it rocks back and forth. This makes the tree bend. When it bends enough, the orangutan can grab the next tree.

Alone in the trees

Orangutans spend nearly all their time in the trees. Young orangutans live with their mothers. Adult **males** nearly always live alone.

▲ *Orangutans do not live in groups like other **great apes**.*

A male makes a long, noisy call. The sound warns other males to keep away. It may also help **females** find a **mate** in the thick forest.

▼ *A male's long call can be heard from far away.*

Orangutan babies

Female orangutans find a **mate** so that they can have babies. Baby orangutans are helpless. Their mothers feed them, carry them, and protect them.

▶▶ *Female orangutans have a baby once every eight years.*

▲ *Babies are carried on their mothers' backs for months.*

The young orangutan will stay with its mother for several years. She will teach it how to find foods that are safe to eat.

Finding food

Orangutans eat many different foods. They like fruit best. They also eat bark, leaves, flowers, and **insects**. They spend most of the day looking for food.

▼ *When they cannot find fruit, orangutans eat plants or insects.*

Different trees make fruit at different times. Orangutans remember when the best trees will have fruit. They make sure to visit these trees when the fruit is **ripe**.

Orangutans will go out of their way to visit a favourite fruit tree.

How orangutans eat

Some forest foods can be tricky to eat. Sharp points protect the fruit of the **durian** tree. An orangutan must work hard to get at its food.

▶▶ *Durians smell awful, but orangutans love the sweet taste.*

A mother orangutan prepares her meal. She throws away seeds and **husks**. Her child watches carefully. It learns which parts of each food are good to eat.

Sometimes a young orangutan takes food from its mother's mouth.

Sleeping nests

As it gets dark, orangutans begin to make nests to sleep in. They make new nests from tree branches each evening.

▲ *Orangutans sometimes make nests for naps during the day.*

When the nests are ready, the orangutans settle in for the night. Young orangutans share nests with their mothers.

Sharing nests with their mothers keeps young orangutans safe.

Rainy season

The rainy season begins late in the year. Heavy rain pours from the sky. Rivers swell. Fewer fruits can be found. Orangutans must eat more bark and leaves.

▼ *Heavy rain keeps the **rainforest** green.*

Most orangutans do not like to get wet.
They make umbrellas out of leaves. They
hold the leaves over their heads to keep
the water off.

*Leaves help orangutans stay dry
when it rains.*

Under attack

Tigers may kill some orangutans. But human hunters are a much bigger problem. Hunters kill orangutan mothers so their babies can be sold as pets.

▲ *Tigers on the **island** of Sumatra may hunt orangutans.*

Each year the **rainforest** gets smaller. Some people cut down its trees to get wood. But many other people are working hard to save the orangutans' forest home.

If we cut down the rainforests, orangutans will have nowhere to live.

Tracker's guide

When you want to watch animals in the wild, you need to find them first. You can look for clues they leave behind.

▶▶ *If you listen carefully, you might hear an orangutan moving through the trees.*

◀◀ A sleeping nest high in a tree means that an orangutan has been here!

⚞ Orangutans can be messy eaters. You might find some dropped food.

29

Glossary

continent the world is split into seven large areas of land called continents. Each continent is divided into different countries.

durian smelly fruit with a hard, thorny shell

equator the pretend line that goes around the centre of the Earth

female animal that can become a mother when it grows up. Women and girls are female people.

great ape one of a group of animals that includes orangutans, chimpanzees, and gorillas

husk dry outer part of some fruits and seeds

insect tiny creature with six legs

island area of land with water all around it

male animal that can become a father when it grows up. Men and boys are male people.

mate when male and female animals produce young

rainforest place where many trees and plants grow close together and where lots of rain falls

ripe ready to eat

Find out more

Books

Asia, Leila Foster (Heinemann Library, 2001)

Animal Life Cycles, Anita Ganeri (Heinemann Library, 2005)

Orangutans, Patricia Kendell (Raintree, 2004)

Hiding in a Rainforest, Patricia Whitehouse
    (Heinemann Library, 2003)

Websites

Visit these websites to find out more amazing facts about
orangutans.

http://www.orangutansonline.com

http://www.pbs.org/wnet/nature/orangutans/

http://www.sandiegozoo.org/animalbytes/t-orangutan.html

Index